SHOAH

Harry Smart was born in Yorkshire in 1956. He was educated at Batley Grammar School and at the University of Aberdeen. His publications include *Criticism and Public Rationality* (Routledge, 1991). His first collection of poems, *Pierrot*, was published by Faber and Faber in 1991. He lives in Montrose, in the north-east of Scotland, and works as a freelance journalist and editor. He is married and has one son.

HARRY SMART

Shoah

**with 'Slow Train to Göttingen'
and translations from Rainer Malkowski's
*Das Meer steht auf***

faber and faber
LONDON · BOSTON

First published in 1993
by Faber and Faber Ltd
3 Queen Square London WC1N 3AU

Photoset by Wilmaset Ltd, Birkenhead, Wirral
Printed in England by Cox & Wyman Ltd, Reading, Berkshire

A CIP record for this book is available from the British Library

ISBN 0-571-16793-4

2 4 6 8 10 9 7 5 3 1

Contents

Slow Train to Göttingen   1

Gatwick – Tegel   3
Die Kontrolle   4
Frohmut   5
Stille Nacht   6
Viktualienmarkt   8
Oisin and the Angels   9
Slow Train to Göttingen   11
Visiting Angelika   12
Würzburg   13
Würzburger Dom   14
Luitpold Arena   15
An Occasion   16
Vier Jahreszeiten   17
Riem – Heathrow   18

Das Meer steht auf   21

Bar Talk   23
The Part and the Whole   24
Round and Round in Circles   25
A Conversation   26
The Engineer's Dream   27
Here Comes the Sea   28

Shoah 29

PART I
The sound of laughter 31
There must be sacrifices 32
Dove's egg 33
The prosecutor states his case 34
The man reads an invitation to his friends 35

PART II
Here are gifts 36
Meanwhile, water says 37
The oaks' dumb decline 38
The salamander 39
Sea's mass 40
Dove embarks 41
Dove warms herself in the ark's kitchen 42

PART III
Spill 43
Neither dove nor crow can hear, but 44
The man says his prayers 45
We sat and counted 46
A quiet day's sailing 47
The man reads a testament 48
Another shipment 50
A memory of white water 51

PART IV
Crow's flight 52
The man is lying in bed 54
The man was anxious 55
It was late 56
The shepherd considers 57

PART V

Sledge-belly   58

The man reviews his aviary   59

Dove sees presents   60

The woman's song   61

Dove takes stock   62

Dove flies higher than she has been before   63

Dove toys unwittingly with heresy   64

PART VI

A second storm   65

The man watches the sea   66

Surely dove is lost   67

PART VII

The horse and its rider   68

The ark sings a lyric   69

Yahweh is a warrior   70

What's left after all this?   71

Notes and Acknowledgements   73

kleine Emailletafeln, die zu einem Gebet auffordern: *Bete für die Seele des Michael O'Neil, der am 17.1.1933 60jährig starb. Bete für die Seele der Mary Keegan, die am 9. Mai 1945 achtzehnjährig starb.*

Heinrich Böll: *Irisches Tagebuch*

Slow Train to Göttingen

Gatwick – Tegel
January 1991

We took off in half-light, the net of fields
still visible in boundaries of gloomy green.
The unlit roads and houses hesitated on the brink

of black. Sunset fell short of apocalyptic
but held our attention long enough for night to fall
below. Towns turned to needlepoint of amber schmuck

while up above we failed to count the stars.
It was raining in Berlin, the terminal fenced off by dark
green-jacketed policemen dealing with a bomb alert.

Die Kontrolle

When Halberstock codified his own
scientific method he explained
the need to establish what would happen
if the key variable were absent,

the need for clarity, kontrollieren,
to check. Since when generations
of scholars have wondered why
they should set up a control and not a check.

False friends; they have trembled at customs,
at the official who wants to see their documents,
er will kontrollieren, their passports,
their own account of who they are and what they've done.

Frohmut

It's August 1955, and my first trip abroad.
It's a trip I still know nothing about
apart from what my mother's told me.
What I remember's constructed

from family memories
of the months before the day
that I was born; the Dambusters
and running from the cinema

to buy a helpless boxer pup, Frohmut;
dark images of bridges and canals,
British lads in Germany, pictures of my mother
carrying me, myself, mein in my precipitating pulp.

Those were the first languages; idealism
blended out of German and English, the hidden
holy orders, gold and white, the head-dress
and the robe I saw unpacked when I was older.

She built bridges, consciously and
subconsciously. I heard voices
that I didn't understand, guessing
a few years later at angels.

Stille Nacht

Lit copper-green against a bluestone sky,
the Holy Ghost towered over
Im Tal's late-nighters and the Kaufhaus
window displays. Rain fell. I checked the map.

On past Alter Peter, past the Strumpf-
Studio, gratings where the darkness
whistled underneath, into Marienplatz,
finished up in Bayerischer Donisl.

Tall young men in lederhosen brought me
Wurst and beer. Sausages swam in their bowl.
I cut into the Weißwurst, remarking to myself
as little as I could, as a man might

when devouring what appeared to be
a bleached penis in the presence
of unchatty skullen Männer each
attending to his own white porcelain dish.

The worst of it is when you've cut
off just one rounded, phallic end;
the sausage droops upon the plate,
publicly unmanned. Rain falls.

I check the dates at intervals,
thirty-six, seventy-two, remembering
the grainy figures, hooded, the Olympic
athletes, coaches, referees, dying in the flat

or on the bus. Somewhere in the friendly fire
'innocence' is the word we need.
What we get instead is introspection,
old men, young men, busy with their meat

or looking at the world along the barrel
of a beer glass. All together now, men
wondering should we have stayed at home,
quivering and solitary, blessing no one.

Viktualienmarkt

Fresh quail, frail handfuls, the hands
of widows scrubbed to dull purple,
heathery meat, cold in polythene,
sweating at dawn.

They couldn't hold a candle to the straw-
berries, red bananas, Indonesian fish-scaled
honey-roasted pear-shapes of Zalugis,
Columbian Apfel-Bananen, Ananas von Kenya,

mangos from Peru and Costa Rica.
They were up against a stall of rabbits
skinned and wearing plastic macs, with
furry slippers on their feet,

rows of cooking fowl, bags
of pigeons. Natürlich sind sie rot,
and wattled yellow, backs the bruisy
colour of the flesh beneath the fingernails.

Zucchini out of Italy with Babafratti,
blind salmon saying their tin last
in air, gaping uselessly, Männchen next
to Weibchen, sexed by the colour

of their flesh, the manly creamy-white
or woman's pink of Karotin still not given
to the eggs. We say goodbye. There are poppies
in their Sommerblüten colours, winterhart.

Oisin and the Angels

If you take the S-Bahn when it's dark,
from Zoo to Friedrichstraße, then look
out to the right as you cross the river
between Bellevue and Lehrter Stadtbahnhof,

you'll see two pink brick angels
walking on the water, and their reflections
broken by the changing surface of the water.
Or if you prefer they're the two piers

of a brick-built bridge, lit from below.
It's not that I expect you to believe in angels,
but understand, I want to hear from heaven:
grace for strangers in a strangers' land.

We look out at the troubled water, Oisin,
Patrick, at a view that's framed in brass.
Or, if you prefer, we could confront together
Luther's bible, neu bearbeitet, gloss

Der Herr is nahe denen, die zerbrochenen
Herzens sind, und hilft denen,
die ein zerschlagenes Gemüt haben.
Der Gerechte muß viel erleiden, aber

There's plenty about angels there as well.
Personally I'm determined to remember
just what I saw, crossing the river
between Bellevue and Lehrter Stadtbahnhof.

And which of us should say boo to the angels
standing with their brick-built arms stretched out,
when all they're trying to do is turn back
sinners from Märchen aus der alten Zeit.

Or, on Oranienburger Straße,
looking with the Kripos at the spattered ground,
the penny-stars of dusty red, the oil-stains,
Which of us should not have pity for

who knows what poor sod who staggered and fell
then dragged himself off to who knows where.
The wandering man whose girth divided suddenly
in the shadow of a church with a belfry made of air

Slow Train to Göttingen
16 January 1991

As we trundled down into the Harz
the sun was setting. Goslar, Seesen, in the glass
reflections of the setting sun, images
bounced between the panes, carriage,
corridor, compartment, setting image

against image. Seven suns met
in the same part of the sky, the direct
and reflected images growing
weaker as the ricochets
each lost a little light.

The train swung round, flexing
its wall of mirrors, turned new angles
to the setting sun, sometimes adding,
sometimes taking images away, grouping
and regrouping them around the centre spot.

Cluster-suns, a storm of suns, images
we travelled with, family of dazzling and dim
discs, some sharp and neat and some diffuse.
Seven suns for a single world of January
landscapes that could be German or Scottish,

either way, northern, cold and hard.
When the seven suns had set
and darkness fell, we gathered speed,
rushing south from Northeim
through a single and inevitable night.

Visiting Angelika
17 January 1991

What I remember of Göttingen is not so much
the half-timbered houses turned to chic shops,
nor eating a president (Ich bin ein Berliner)
full of jam, nor an Amerikaner, but the cold

clear light, students gathering round the Gänseliesel
that I never kissed, the ring of arms around the town,
the ice and the earthen walls we walked
together listening to the sound of running water

echoing on frozen water. 'Häppy Borstei Lars!'
the spray-paint can had written on
a moderately historic wall. We never found
the water mill. All the signs were there,

Kein Blut für Öl. You wore a white bandage
round your arm for peace. We shopped for music,
listened to Sam Cooke singing 'Wonderful World',
then slept. Me in your bed, you upstairs.

Würzburg

Riemenschneider's Philip, stony
man fat as a frog with a bull-croak
throat. Blank-eyed wooden Barbara

with a wooden cup, collecting the facts
from an arrow-shot Sebastian calmly
facing her as if he were bored, merely

waiting for a bus or enduring the slow
marrow-hunt, the woodworm larvae
burrowing in his bones. Finally,

Maria mit Kind, aus dem Grabfeld,
bald and earless, mother and child
rotted together. Nothing links her

wrist to her elbow, the child's armless.
Both Maria's hands are disembodied,
carefully clasping what remains of the Christ

child to her shattered chest. An accident
of grain has been exploited by the wind
and rain; her head is cloven as a hoof

from crown to lower jaw. Es gibt auch
einen Christus auf dem Palmesel. Der Esel hat
seine beiden Augen; beim Christus fehlt eine Hand.

Würzburger Dom

There is a little cloister in the Dom
in Würzburg, off the tourist track
of altars and Figuren. When the rain
swills down in June, washing the cloister
clean of dust and fallen leaves, the birds
take shelter underneath the arches
or beneath a false acacia with tender leaves.

All around the cloister, against the wall,
are gravestones, mediaeval faces
indecipherable. Two birds glide
down from the roof to rest in the fresh wet
courtyard. Two pigeons purr, a dog whines
in the middle distance like an unoiled wheel
slowly turned by hand.

Luitpold Arena

Ein Paar Würste und kaltes Bier
from the Imbiss beside the lake.
Ein lauter amerikanischer Hubschrauber
hacks across the choppy water.

Hinter den säulenlosen Tribünen spielen
the boys and girls, tennis, plocking
gelbe Bälle gegen die bleibenden Mauern.
Mercedes and Bay-Em-Vays cruise by.

Man kann auf der Stelle stehen, auf der
Ich-kenne-den-Menschen-nicht once stood. The wind
weht irgendwo. Was man sagt, hört fast niemand,
so long as you whisper. Sit and pray,

vielleicht hören die Götter, vielleicht
a time like that won't come again.
Zwei Autos parken. Zwei Paare steigen aus
and climb slowly up the pale stone steps. One

der Frauen ist unglaublich schön, mit goldnem Haar
and golden legs that part her long green skirt
bei jedem Schritt. Man muß immer folgen,
but she's eventually lost to sight.

An Occasion

für Jorge Joao Gomondai
Ostersonntag 1991, Dresden

An occasion for sculling races,
Nürnberg fertig, Bamberg fertig,
Würzburg fertig? As I walked round
the Kongressbau I heard the stations called,

Achtung, a shot, the crowd called out
for victory. Down by the water something smelled
rotten. The officials' launch churned by
and into the distance. Suddenly a commotion

of reeds and lilies at the water's edge waved
and slapped as the wake came finally to the shore.

Vier Jahreszeiten

On the Maximilianstraße: I was just. I was very just
round the corner von dem Haus des alten Rechtsgelehrten
where, still unknown, his 35jährige daughter had stayed
all her life in a hidden room, clawing what bare wood

she could reach at the end of her tether. The naked
there was: there; leather tether, narrow bed of bare
metal mit dreckverschmierten bodybelts, the old
contemptible, inevitable piss, shit and decay.

So they loved their little Tochter
obwohl sie 'sehr sehr geisteskrank war',
liebten ihre kleine Tochter,
Tochter 'einfach nicht ansprechbar'.

Yesterday we were in the Vier Jahreszeiten
courtesy of the laptop maker. The PR people
and their clients were buying the drinks,
Tosh, whatever, however many, for as long as

there was: us, wanting and having a night of it.
Heute sind sie weg, I'm out on the street I am,
struck by a strange tongue-tongue I am
as a stranger always is, not always grasping.

Tonight I dined in the Ratskeller, asked
and answered in alien syllables, fast unsprechbar.
Tonight I dined in the Ratskeller, eating up
my chicken dinner, wie ein echter Rechtsgelehrter.

Riem – Heathrow

From up here, I can tell you,
the cloud looks terrific, un-
symbolic, and I feel damn fine.
In Club Europe class I've just been
served wine, smoked salmon, veal, and

feine Trüffel-Praline from Rausch.
I'm sipping my Drambuie
and I feel damn fine. Someone else
is paying. The suffering is elsewhere.
The sun slides over my tray like a jelly.

The coast is miles below, plain strand,
no waves, land and sea sunk in the same
sunlit cigarette-smoke Blaugrau.
The ships aren't moving, still wakes
glisten on the water.

The first time I saw the Friedensengel
I almost cried. Now I can see the waves.
Now I wish the whole dim world were
silly, were not going to hell in a handcart.
But I'm not losing sight of the waves

nor of the serpent-headed rivers
on their own courses. Oilseed rape's
a Van Gogh, rooflights glitter;
we'll be on the ground in fifteen minutes.
Mozart whispers from the speakers overhead.

We bank and turn, a stream winks
into heliograph, silver cars run like mice,
a powerboat writes sunny thumbprints
on the reservoir. This is one of those
journeys that you finish on your own.

Das Meer steht auf

Translations of poems from *Das Meer steht auf*
by Rainer Malkowski

Bar Talk

The lake, like lead, talks
about itself with gently sloshing waves.
Alongside, the empty tables and chairs
plastered with chestnut leaves
talk about empty tables and chairs.
First impressions are
the whole story –
despite the endless, unhesitating
cues for entry or response:
the lake to the cool of the day,
empty tables and chairs giving
an opening to autumn.
And the insect trap in the tree,
a cage with a lifeless neon tube,
throws out a line to the summer
night bright with wine and talk.

The Part and the Whole

I learned a wee bit today.

In the evening, when the lad fetched
the horses from the field
– one white, one brown one,
one black pony trotting along behind –
I tried to memorize
the clatter of hooves on asphalt;

The hooves against the other noises,
the noises against the smells,
the noises and smells
against the shapes and colours.

I'll never have to say:
I've kept the world
too carelessly
in mind.

Round and Round in Circles

Late at night, standing by the window –
counting faraway stars
and considering
old systems.

Resolutions.

Then a car starts up
nearby, returns
an awkward silence.

A Conversation

A conversation –
ok, but what about?
Try the newspaper,
the colour of the lady doctor's hair.
Did you ever have luck like that
in all your life?
No, you don't ask that kind of thing.
Lovely day, isn't it – yesterday
wasn't half as nice.
A drip. A monitor. A
finally steady
line along the screen.

The Engineer's Dream

Then this room, he said
when we were looking round the house,
and he showed us a padded door;
I haven't been in here for years.
The furniture's not been moved,
the shutters are still down.
Scream all you like, from the outside,
no-one in here will hear a thing.
Even when I'm dead,
in this room
nothing will have changed.

Here Comes the Sea

Night time, surf storm:
over the promenade,
in among the trees.

Atlantic smash
in the canopy.

Here comes the sea,
leaf-green wave on wave.

This is a reinterpretation of 'Das Meer steht auf',
the title poem of Malkowski's collection.

Shoah

Du siehst, die Sorgen lassen einem keine Zeit für persönliche freie und frohe Stunden. Der Kopf ist voll von unruhigen und furchtbaren Gedenken, und ich habe gar kein Interesse mit jemandem zusammen zu kommen . . .

Bleibe gesund, mein Liebes, wir können ja nicht ändern, wir müssen alles durchmachen.
Ich küsse Dich innigst, Deine Jettel.

Charlotte Rosenthal

PART I

The sound of laughter

A man watches his son
Walk towards him with a bride,
All smiles. She wears a bonny dress,
He likes her, wonders about her family, says nothing.

Soon he will have the blessing of grandchildren.
It seems almost corrupt
Judgment; the crown cracks. *Schachath*.
The old man smiles at the blue sky,

Greets his son, his icon, smiles at the girl.
Her face is round as an egg,
Her belly fragile. He considers
Prospects. He hears the storm coming, he says.

No one worries, no one dares
To believe what they hear or even what they see.
Blindness is cold charity.
It's time for images

Without the prompt of artefact, memories
For an empty world. It's time to gather in
Sheep and goats, crow and the dove,
Sons and daughters and the sound of laughter.

There must be sacrifices

The connoisseur takes his razor,
Knows exactly what he's doing,

Slowly, dripping just the right amount into the cup
He will drink. Jade remedy, the ruby vintage

Drowns his sorrows. One by one
His images break. He unmakes himself.

Dove's egg

Light penetrates the egg,
The membrane shines within the shell.

Coiled potential struggles
All around the little globe.

Sticky calcite fragments glisten.
Birth is commonplace.

The prosecutor states his case

I have flown the earth;
I have leapt to claim my own.

I am bright in sunlight,
Darkness in deep places.

I saw, in those first days,
The gold and the onyx,

I know the scent of aromatic resins,
The sweet river airs were mine, before

That whirling sword
Touched my heart.

Now I am become my true free self,
May take the stage, may roar and fall

Upon the sons of men
As *winter, pitiless*.

My time is short, I have only a season, but how
Fantastically I carry off the light.

The man reads an invitation to his friends

Drink this cup,
Drink it, or my hospitality is ended.
He views the scalding brew.
Listen, drink, or die of a deeper draught.

He turns to his assistant;
Take this cup. Take it to the kings in high places,
To rulers, princes,
All of them.

Make them drink.
They will not drink?
They will drink this cup,
They will drink this deeper cup.

He breaks the bottle,
Pours the dark wine down the street,
Filling sewers. Gutter-loving, dark wine overflows
The pavement of judgment right to the palace door.

The cup is bottomless, the flood it looses
Rushes like a dam-burst through the alleys,
Ginnels, closes, wynds,
It drowns mall, avenue, crescent.

Gilded arcades are washed as urine-spattered stairways,
Reek of ammonia, stale food, sweat, are washed down.
This cup washes and fills winos and kings.
Look, he says, they're drinking.

PART II

Here are gifts

Fruit, wheat, milk.
Here are gifts of strength and skill,
Of husbandry and artifice.

Make of them what you will,
I ask only gratitude,
That you remember who it was that gave them.

So, said the man, we were led to believe.
So we understood our God's naivety.
So it was.

But what did you expect? You made us
Agents of your grace, fit-to-judge angels
With gifts of gold, iron, ore and forge.

And I am made minstrel for it all
With rye bread, bitter heart and few friends,
All for your gifts of good things.

Well, we are one in this, my judge,
That all this glittering tray of gifts
Be cast upon the waters.

This gently falling rain will bring no harvest from the fields,
Quite right. You have made your judgment known,
Now let it fall.

Meanwhile, water says

The quenching of fires is my delight,
In all places where there are fires –
Then hiss, and sizzle, I bring quenched coals.

I see a single man, distant, heat the iron,
I hear the stroke and see the metal flinch.
The armourer says he knows my joy in quenching

The flamy yellow blade,
Hearing the metal bite and spit, all trough-gulp,
I drowned him with a laugh.

I quench all heat, all appetite,
I satisfy with tumult.

The oaks' dumb decline

The false autumn's branches, bare crops
Whipping the school sky
That stings them with cold rain,
They don't know that this time
Is beyond petulance. It is too serious.

Everyone tends to become better
At what it is they think they need to do –
Always assuming that they survive,
As these still sappy stalwarts won't.
There they go, titanic trunks,

Lost branches, earth rinsing
From an archaeology of roots.

The hillside turned into a muddy slipway
And down we went.

The salamander

Climbs webwet towards a high cave.

Claws clatter. Shale fractures,
Spins down the mountainside. Rinsed
From stone, sinking, drowned
Families accommodate themselves to Schlamm.

The salamander deposits himself, high terrestrial detritus.
Whumf and smack of water crash.
The rock-throat nozzle forces
Paste of despair.

Beneath a final quietness of water
Grey silicates pack silent voices. Mineral,
The salamander turns to stone, preserved,
Poor flood-man, for an age of faith.

Sea's mass

Sea's mass is clumsy,
Wrestling with hills and parapets
On broken glass. *Kyrie*

Sea's mass is an alarm of gongs
Untempled, bell-beat of confession.
The face that matters is occluded. *Kyrie*

Counterpoint in pastoral
Fails to register. Fires are finally extinguished.
Hosannas lose a little in translation. *Kyrie eleison*

A deluge of preachers fell
Roaring, then silence.
Who would dream such flailing silences

Could echo to anyone's glory?
As the waters cover the sea and the cries,
The cries have died, the word is, Be still.

Dove embarks

Evening's ink,
A rising tide that
Set the sealed hull in mud-suck,
Pitch dark shining in the moon's dim view.

Dove flew at a narrow sluice way;
Wine-wrung
Crow was there before her.
She saw his legs' scratch and angled

Spurt of effort, crow scraped the wood,
Hatched through, cleared the opening.
Dove thought in tatters,
If that crow could hardly make it

How can I?
Timbers crushed her dark labour
At the needle's eye. It will kill me
If I push any harder I will break.

A hand gripped her neck,
Pull, but the fingers found her body,
Held her tight and through she popped.
Gladly caged.

Dove warms herself in the ark's kitchen

Looking at the oven
Dove considers the warmth of it, the silence
Of the iron within which the fire burns,
The iron stability of fact.

She turns and watches the timbers
Not moving one against the other, unresisting
As a nail is thumped into the hull to hold a coat.
She is glad of this shelter, of this dry, warm place

Which offers her neutrality, used for kindness.
She is glad of wood pushed unresisting into fire.
This place had a rough making and a launching
Without prayers for blessing. This place sailed out

On clawing desperation, on total bitterness,
And now it sails, it is observed,
No more.
Beyond the hull the water is observed

To be gentle, though Dove has heard hymns
Of violence, taken its heart to be demonic.
Dove sees the man sitting at the table
Silently, incapable of action, simply being what he is.

PART III

Spill

A spill of light,
Sun's inspection,
Flooded the decks.
Our faces
Stood clear
To one another's sight.

Neither dove nor crow can hear, but

The pit has a deep voice,
All cries are lost within it.
Pillars and colonnades, dead jaws, ornamental
Ponds release their lampreys to a royal banquet.

How many valleys folded their sides together?
This one did: see how the scree tumbled.
These do not belong together, rock and robes,
Fine silver and the oak tree, cradle and brazier.

This conglomerate
Sits metastable, anaerobic.
Flesh decays, hollows form and fill
With silt, gradually cemented, or collapse;

Turbidite sequences slip and rush,
Greywacke settles
So slow. Quick, listen; so
slow . . . slow.

Already, in the wet charnel,
Roots worked. Xylem and phloem
Sent nectar messages silently
From cell to cell.

The man says his prayers

You have said, *maybe*
I will pour out a blessing
That you cannot contain.

You have said, *you soar like the eagle*
And make your nest among the stars
But you cannot escape me.

Your deluge has sheathed swords
In mud with spears, ploughs and pruning hooks
But this damn world's still angry, still at war.

You have said, *rend your hearts*
And not your garments. But my heart, well, let's just call it
Broken. It will not work. I cannot change myself.

You have strength for this probably
Stony dissection. Reconstruction seems beyond
Hope. Perhaps one day you'll specialize in dry bones.

Perhaps. One day the bones you've broken will rejoice,
One day there'll be joy in heaven,
Peace on earth, goodwill to all men.

Each evening the man led his family in worship,
Held out his arms in a blessing
Called benediction.

We sat and counted

We sat and counted, gave them their own names,
Those that we remembered, we tried to give them names.
We tried to give them colour for their hair, their eyes,
We gave them credit for the things they'd said,
We told the stories we remembered.

No-one knew his name, that boy
Who sailed his voice sky high
Above a small boat on a quiet river.
We'd heard him often, wondered why he sang
Such lovely songs and seemed so still.

We'd made his song a cabaret.
Now we made a festival in transit.
We'd watched him on the silent water, witnessing
His anonymity, how well he sang. Now, running
Out of names, we travelled for the most part silently.

A quiet day's sailing

The air's fly-warm.
Scuppers fertilise the day's
Salt furrow. Mad ploughing, gulls follow.
No warriors call.

We are all a little frightened of violence, now.
There are no wars to sail to, no coasts,
No proud walls tall against the sky
But this grey depth.

Pastures are gone far below the keel.
The man shudders, only the serpent could tell him
That they are passing over the abyss.
Even the mountains drowned some time ago.

The man reads a testament

He watched, as it had become a habit,
The flotsam drifting by the boat,
Last messages from home
After home, sending their mundane properties
Out upon the water, blind,
Not waiting for any return.

The man had made himself
A fishhook for a world
Of goods, if they caught his eye he pulled them up,
Inspected them, these offerings to his God.
He would not keep them, for they were dedicated.
He would look, consider, throw them back.

There was a flask; he'd fished it out and opened it,
Taboo. He found a document within. He read,
Returned the flask but kept the document
Hidden, not daring let his family see
The lamplight far into the night,
Reading, over and over,

We are all alive, save our father.
We have begged the waves for mercy,
So great is our fear, but still they advance.
We can go no higher; by evening,
If the water knows no compassion, we will be dead.
We had prayed, and in the last hours
We have begged the waves for mercy.

The man kept station in the bow.
He leant towards the water,
His face turned from his family.
He dared not let his family see
He wept
Late tears of intercession.

Another shipment

We'd fed well, that day, burnt offerings, no joke.
The roasted meat and carefully cellared wine, broken
Bread made conversation flow for once around the table
Where we quarantined ourselves while all the world hung
Out its yellow flag – yellow sun trailing our thin line of smoke.

The woman made us pay attention to a shadow on the water
Just too far away to tell what it might be. We thought
At first a storm was gathering, but the waves' direction
Made a meeting with what soon became a chain of boats,
Barges, low and heavy, quiet, no sign of activity on board.

We hadn't seen so much as scattered timbers of another vessel
Since the Sabbath. Then our hope of seeing anyone's survival
Fell, we thought, a final time. This latest transport
Seemed untouched by storm or violence, its waterline
Must surely mean a thousand souls or more within each hold.

So there were, at least, and as our boat drew close there came
The choking, inevitable smell of their decay. Jammed
Too tight against each other, desperate resettling, the heat
And filth had throttled them, every one, six thousand
Of them slave-packed into floating graves. We sang Amen

Of yet another Kaddish, prayed for strangers once again,
Wondering how it was that only flies survived. Grain
Stored in our vessel, it lacked flavour. We prayed for storms
To sink that silent train of dead. We wondered who had
Watched the barges leaving harbour, frail tears in the rain.

A memory of white water

We passed through water whitened
By almond blossom,
By branches white with almond blossom
Torn from the trees'
Last flowering for funeral.

I remembered how my God had said
You will see how harshly,
You will see how harshly
I deal with all my enemies
Who say they do not know me.

I remember how I wondered
Who is my neighbour now?
Who is my neighbour now
That I have no one but my family
Who say they do not know me?

PART IV

Crow's flight

Who is black as an ark?
Crow is. All external, all sense
Sealed and armoured.
Crow wears black and proud of it.
But this flood goads him,
The archetype iconoclast outclassed.

Grit beneath the clouds' lid
Flies crow.
Water on the brain, he circles the ark,
Sees flies drawn by sewage
To the ark as if it were a beacon of shit.
He sees them grub and seethe over the hull,

A second skin.
He clacks his beak, swoops in for a fat insect,
Gollops it down.
Take more than a flood to get rid of old crow.
He sees a mat of kelp and apple, wrack and grape
Stones floating, water swarming;

The worms have not drowned.
Ripe flesh rots, sweet, skins peel.
Crow's claws release a vegetable pus.
He scrambles, treachery
Slips him from a fruitskin,
Oil of feathers flicking greasy weeds.

This raft is too damn thin, all stalks.
Damn! No prey, his pinions beseech
The mouldering wash.
Salt has not preserved this harvest.
Crow sulks and flies the flotsam trap,
Wet spite-rocket.

The man is lying in bed

It's a warm, sunny morning; calm seas.
His bed is warm, he's relaxed.
He watches the room's light through closed eyelids,
Sees his own translucent flesh and blood.

He's still half-asleep, watching the world through his eyelids.
He sees the ark, its waterline
A skim of trailing branches,
Leaves float past, a black feather.

He knows he cannot see it.
He knows his eyelids are closed.
He knows the world is as he understands it,
Empty, calm, and with the sun shining on it.

The man was anxious

He had waited for a long time,
Scanning the wide horizon.
As he sat at meat
He listened for scratching claws
On roof-tile or window-board
But heard only water slapping pitch.

He smelled the spray,
Salt and bitterly
Refreshing, flushing out the dung-smell
Of the relics that sailed with him
Breeding food for his table,
Sharing his grain and water.

Such a washing and we are not yet clean,
He thought, watching
His family
Snapping at each other round the table.
Roasted bones, brittle, he broke
A rib of lamb between his hands.

It was late

Evening in the kitchen. I sat quietly
Beside the stove and fed the child. Just
The two of us still awake, the air clear of piety
And silences. I heard him breathing,

Felt the healthy suck of him at me,
His toothless confidence of feeding. We'd struggled
Through weeks of cracked skin till we learned
Together how to manage this.

He'd learned. He reckoned nothing to it now.
He reckoned nothing to totality, nothing
To the spirit of the age, but he'd learned
To hold my hand and stand on his own two feet.

He broke from feeding, milk-drops on his lips, smiling
At me. That same day, in the new summer weather
We'd watched this boy's father
Take his own life in his hands.

We'd watched him dive into the sea, watched
His white flesh nail itself to darkness
Underneath the water, disappearing
For that moment when time stopped

And no-one said a thing. We cheered him
As he surfaced, as he waved. We laughed
Because we didn't know what else to do
And cried when he had climbed on board again.

The shepherd considers

A sunset, he remembers
That last night's false sky,
Black bulk at his shoulder, dwarfing him.
Now almost everyone's asleep.

Tonight the washed world
Holds no dust to the setting sun,
No angry sky. Even the waves are quiet,
Clean air wraps him.

Silhouette horizon.
The fire is quenched.
Cool, cool,
In the morning he will release the dove.

My God, how would a sunset look now?
Such an unbroken horizon, such expanse
To shine like blood.
The shepherd leans towards his own reflection.

PART V

Sledge-belly

Churns the water. His broad gut is a threshing board,
Studded, see the gleaming metal in his hide.
Leviathan has not drowned.

See that boat;
Leviathan's tail, hooked to grapple,
Swings beneath the keel.

Dove is afraid of the gulls,
Glad to be well away from them.
Those first moments' flight were scary

But the gulls seem not to notice her.
Dove turns to watch the distant boat,
Sees the gulls' sudden scattering.

Surely that's not the boat's shadow?
Dove wonders what has sent the gulls away
Screeching. Salt

Blood, tears and vitreous
Humour, dove anatomy and physiology
Lift her well clear of the water.

The man reviews his aviary

Survivors; this godwit bird, small,
By scholars' standards silly,
Has a life-time's worth of categories
Hidden from the knife.

All the world's gone mudflat
Under brackish water; brine-
Dilute, the salt has lost its savour,
The waves have trodden it underfoot.

Yolk and albumen of seabirds' eggs
Are mixed with clay, white feathers
Of a novel sediment settling in fragile fantails,
Broken hulls. Sudden sights of absence

Unannounced, stimulating unexpected senses
Of the unrecoverable wings that never flew,
Families hidden in generalities that pass for whole
Identities; crow, owl, duck, gull, hawk and dove.

Denied the shallows, dunlin tolerate the ark,
Sadly, clipped and pinioned. They'll not beat
The air again and must mate for sheer survival
Of the species, of the race.

Held within the ark's pale and seedy light
They watch the first clutch, anxious parents
Hoping that their children will be able
To fly away from them.

Dove sees presents

Scattered on the waves.
There must be gods of the waves here, she says,

For I have seen such offerings before,
And worse. These gods have taken to themselves

Such an orgy of worship,
Such a welter of rich gifts

That surely there can never be another.
This is a worship to end all worship.

The woman's song

One day the woman sang.
Her voice was shining as the sun on water
And the water calm around us as a stone,
Unflowing, so it seemed. No wind, no sigh, no call of birds.

She walked out of the kitchen and along the deck
Towards the bow. She moved as gracefully as water
Cleanly poured into a silver bowl,
The sunlight on her hair, silver, her face a stone.

She sang as winter sings in heaven,
Cold and clear, the song she sang was rime
Of quietness still-grown, still-born.
We never wished to hear that song again.

It was lovely as only sea and sky are lovely.
As only sea and sky had terrified us with their emptiness
The woman silenced us. We watched her and we listened,
We looked at the horizon and wondered why she sang.

Afterwards, the woman sleeping, all the rest of us
Discussed her song and tried to recollect the words,
In vain. Her song had lodged like ice within our hearts,
Quite apart from words.

Dove takes stock

The world is becalmed,
The waves have learned to whisper, *Ruach*,
Gentle at last. Now the sea's a perfect mirror to heaven

But dove has the sky freehold.
Below: cylinders, pyramids, cubes,
Irregular shards;

Schools of sea snakes
Thread a stony framework, shoals
Fragment, their lines track currents.

Wrasse, tang and surgeon
Probe. Such bonny colours
Powder blue the muds.

Dove sighs, and sees her pale breast
Dull, soft, hard-worked.
She's growing tired.

Dove flies higher than she has been before

Dove spires to heaven, so she thinks,
Searching for earth.

She hardly dares look up or down.
Dove sits weathervane,

A small moon, just sundust this morning.
The cold air sharpens her wings, she is a dove-knife,

A wind-sword.
Her glance constructs an equator,

Splits the globe.
In her head a needle pulls,

She spreads her wings and glides.
Dove treads blue wounds, dark heaven and drowned earth.

Dove toys unwittingly with heresy

Dove has meditated on the fragile shell,
Has seen a dove's egg broken,
But she cannot describe her own contents. Well,

She has listened often enough to the old man's prayers,
Not comprehending *nephesh* and temples,
Life, hope, materiality. She rests;

A sent wave splashes her wing.
She shakes the water from her feathers,
Looks up, sees that the mist is lifting.

She opens her wing and considers each quill,
Light and air pass through
Yet there is a membrane still.

Dove considers the mist, stares at it,
Sees it thin to mere invisibility.
Thin, says dove, as the Holy Spirit.

PART VI

A second storm

Dove has been gone, it seems like years.
The man remembers a walk;

Four friends beside a river,
It chattered pleasantly as they spoke.

It said, *chesed, chesed*,
And sang gently.

But all night long his lullaby has failed
To hush the rising storm.

His gentle memories have grown thorns,
His gentle stream has become a fierce nation.

Grace has endured the winter,
Now it runs in spate.

All that day the ark was driven
Through the storm's veins.

The man watches the sea

The holocaust is not complete
Until this black log rolls a few more
Remnants overboard. He fears

Bad nights.
Water tests the man's construction.
It's a hard judge. Hear it rap on the boards.

Yet we are kings, he thinks,
I rule this world. Monarch of all
He surveys his lands.

His walls forbid him everything but fear,
Grey battering boundaries, boulders;
Water flexes its muscles. His mountain hunt him.

Surely dove is lost

In this night, night
Of storms.

By first light the water is calm,
Diminishing,

Windows open to a quiet wind,
Voices return to their usual level.

The man glances from time to time at the sill,
Hoping that no-one will notice him looking.

Dove lands almost silently
Carrying a small branch.

The man rises and takes the dove gently,
He warms her.

Dove and the man look at each other,
The branch is held between them.

The silent question is
What are we going to do with this, then?

He lays the branch down on the table, the sacrament
Ready, but the altar still to be built.

Dove returns to her cage, and the man to his
Hard chair.

PART VII

The horse and its rider

I will sing to the Lord for he is highly exalted,
The horse and its rider he has cast into the sea.
The King's chariots and his army he has cast into the sea.
The finest of the King's officers are drowned in the Great Sea.
The deep waters covered them;
They sank to the depths like a stone.

You have destroyed the army of the oppressor, O Lord,
You have consumed multitudes of the oppressed.
In your unfailing love you will lead the people you have
redeemed.
In your strength you will guide them to your holy dwelling.
The nations will hear and tremble;
Terror and dread will fall upon them.

The Lord will reign for ever and ever;
Before him no god was formed, nor will there be one after
him.
No-one can deliver out of his hand.
When he acts, who can reverse it?

The ark sings a lyric

Years have gone by since I was cut
From the deep holt
And made into a spectacle
Men laughed at, set high on a hill.

Now there are only those I hold,
And those I love.
They will leave me empty
When this journey is fulfilled.

**Until then I am their kingdom
And will protect**
Their spirit and flesh
Until this journey is fulfilled.

My roots are torn, the folk I hold
Will soon set down
And build a city. Until then
I am their city and their city wall.

Yahweh is a warrior

He sets his bow in the heavens' tiller,
Shows his fire-bright war-bow
Arc, taut.

Such arrows that bow would cast,
Says the man,
Though aimed at heaven.

He bows his head,
This water has been like coals to his mouth.
So he has been favoured. He has survived.

I will not destroy the world again,
Says the message,
By water.

Dove, light-ringed, is free at last;
She circles from the ark
But turns to look back

From the distance.
The boat is a hollowed skull
Charred and swollen. *Metanoia*;

Jewelled breath, sunlit dew.
New meadows hear
Dove's wood-flute call.

What's left after all this?

More sea than land. Fewer boundaries
And family ties divide the world;
All earth's folk are one. A joke at last.
If ever there are wise folk perhaps
They'll take the time to watch the sea,
To study waves, to learn to be quiet.

Meanwhile I'll show you a man at work;
A bald bespectacled man working
For all he's worth, laying leather
Time and again in the guillotine.
His eye never leaves the point
Where the steel cuts through the stuff.

In this man's city are eight yards of names
Engraved very, very small on metal plates,
The columns of characters two yards tall;
Adler, Badmann, Eichbaum, Gans,
Lion, Rosenbaum and Wolf; a carnival
Of creatures, eagles, oak-trees, geese.

The Hart pants after cooling streams,
The Lion lies down with the Lamm.
There's even Hamlet, Julie, 21. 07. 74 geboren,
Verschollen, Minsk. The last yard's blank
For those lost wonders of the world, the Golden
Peccabile, the Verschwundene Luft.

NOTES AND ACKNOWLEDGEMENTS

Poems from this collection previously appeared in the following magazines, whose editors I would like to thank: *Lines Review, Chapman, Outposts, Oxford Poetry, Times Literary Supplement, Stand Magazine.* I am particularly grateful to Tessa Ransford, Director of the Scottish Poetry Library, and to Angelika Dräger and Graziana Goldwurm, for their assistance.

I am happy to acknowledge the support of the Scottish Arts Council, who gave me a writer's bursary in 1991 when I was finalising the manuscript of this book.

The picture on the cover, by an unknown artist, was done in Terezín (Theresienstadt) in 1943 or 1944. It was produced in drawing classes held in secret by Friedl Dicker-Brandeis, a Bauhaus architect who was held for a time in Terezín before, on 6 October 1944, she was deported to Auschwitz, where she was killed. I am grateful to the Jewish Museum in Prague for permission to reproduce the picture.

Slow Train to Göttingen

'Oisin and the angels'
Oranienburger Straße: the location of the main synagogue in pre-war Berlin.

'Luitpold Arena'
One of the remaining sections of the Reichsparteitagsgelände at Nürnberg.

'An Occasion'
Jorge Joao Gomondai: a Gastarbeiter from Mozambique. On Easter Sunday 1991 he was thrown from a moving tram by a group of neo-Nazis. He died later in hospital. The Kongressbau is part of the Reichsparteitagsgelände.

Das Meer steht auf

These poems are selected from *Das Meer steht auf*, by Rainer Malkowski, published by Suhrkamp Verlag, Frankfurt, 1989. The translations appear by permission of Suhrkamp Verlag, who hold all rights to *Das Meer steht auf*. I am grateful to both Rainer Malkowski and Martine Oepping at Suhrkamp for their cooperation and assistance.

Shoah

Work on this sequence was under way before the first showing on British television of Claude Lanzmann's film *Shoah*. However, the impact of this film on the development of my sequence was considerable, and I would like to record my sense of indebtedness to Claude Lanzmann for his work. Much of his film's influence on my book has been indirect, but I have alluded to some particular passages from the film, for example in the poem 'We sat and counted'.

The text by Charlotte Rosenthal is from a letter preserved in the Jewish Museum, housed in the Martin-Gropius-Bau in Berlin: *You see, worries don't leave any room for privacy or happiness. My head is full of unsettledness and terrible thoughts, and I just don't want to get together with other people . . . Keep well, my love, we can't change anything, we just have to get through it all.*
With all my love, Jettel

'The horse and its rider'
This is based on a collage of references from Exodus and from Isaiah, using the New International Version, a modern translation of the Bible published by Hodder. The majority of the text is taken from the NIV, but with adaptations and interpolations.

'What's left after all this?'
The names are taken from the Holocaust Memorial in the Jewish Museum in Frankfurt.